dôNrm´-lä-püsl

dôNrmˊ-lä-püsl
from the *joan of arc* project

kari edwards
edited by Tina Žigon

eth press
kuwait city · toronto
boston · cincinnati

dôNrm'-lä-püsl © 2017 Fran Blau, © 2003 kari edwards.
Introduction and notes © 2017 Tina Žigon

This work is licensed under a Creative Commons Attribution-NonCommercial 4.0 International License. To view a copy of this license, visit: http://creativecommons.org/licenses/by-nc/4.0/ or send a letter to Creative Commons, 444 Castro Street, Suite 900, Mountain View, California, 94041, USA.

This edition published in 2017 by
eth press
an imprint of punctum books
ethpress.com | punctumbooks.com

eth press is a parascholarly poetry press interested in publishing innovative poetry that is inspired by, adapted from, or otherwise inhabited by medieval texts.

eth press is an imprint of punctum books, an open-access and print-on-demand independent publisher dedicated to radically creative modes of intellectual inquiry and writing across a whimsical para-humanities assemblage.

David Hadbawnik, Chris Piuma, Dan Remein, and Lisa Ampleman are the editors of eth press, and we can be contacted at ethpress [at] gmail.com. We are currently accepting proposals and submissions.

ISBN-10: 0692374515
ISBN-13: 978-0692374511
LCCN: 2017951817

Cover and book design: Chris Piuma.
Cover art: Omar Al-Nakib, "Small Adlib no. 4."

introduction
"ready to do battle with proverbs and pronouns"
an introduction to kari edwards' *dôNrmˊ-lä-püsl*

> "To me, gender is a poetry each of us makes
> out of the language we are taught."
> —Leslie Feinberg, *Trans Liberation:*
> *Beyond Pink or Blue*

Why are we are still so fascinated by Joan of Arc? In her recent book *Joan of Arc: A Life Transfigured*, Kathryn Harrison offers one possible answer:

> The tension between truth and fiction continues to quicken Joan's biography, for a story, like a language, is alive only for as long as it changes. Latin is dead. Joan lives. She has been imagined and reimagined by Shakespeare, Voltaire, Schiller, Twain, Shaw, Brecht, Anouilh, and

thousands of writers of less renown. Centuries after her death, she has been embraced by Christians, feminists, French nationalists, Mexican revolutionaries, and hairdressers, her crude cut inspiring the bob worn by flappers as a symbol of independence from patriarchal strictures. Her voices have held the attention of psychiatrists and neurologists as well as theologians. It seems Joan of Arc will never be laid to rest. Is this because stories we understand are stories we forget? (16)[1]

Harrison's question suggests that even after centuries have passed since Joan of Arc lived, and even after numerous retellings of her story, it lives on because there is still something unfathomable about it. Readers return to the story because Joan, even after all the social change that has occurred since her times, is still a complex and mysterious heroine — courageous, unwavering in her faith and love for her country, unshaken in her determination to do what her voices are telling her to do. But if the readers' interest can be explained, what is it about her story that makes writers keep retelling it?

Perhaps Joan's story is a way for authors to tell their own stories. In her study of various versions of Joan of Arc, Ann Astell focuses on the concept of authorship.[2] Discussing some of the early adaptations (Paul Claudel's libretto *Jeanne d'Arc au bûcher* (scored by Arthur Honegger), Christine de Pizan's *Le Ditié de Jehanne d'Arc*, and Robert Southey's *Joan of Arc*), Astell locates the beginning of these retellings in what

---

1 Kathryn Harrison, *Joan of Arc: A Life Transfigured* (New York: Doubleday, 2014).

2 Ann W. Astell, *Joan of Arc and Sacrificial Authorship* (Notre Dame: University of Notre Dame Press, 2003).

she calls "authorial identification with Joan of Arc" (4). She writes,

> What is striking about Jehannine fictions is the way Joan's portrayal varies from work to work, each time mirroring the life and "death" of the author. To the extent that Joan is made to resemble the author who recreates her, she attests to the importance of biographical criticism and to the thought of the poets, playwrights, essayists, and novelists who conceived of her in an imaginary relationship to themselves, identifying with her. (8)

I suggest that kari edwards' Joan of Arc stems from this same identification. As a transgender woman, edwards could identify with Joan. Further, edwards' retelling of Joan's story not only rekindles interest in Joan's legacy, but also ensures that the language used to tell her story keeps changing to stay in step with changing times. As transgender issues continue moving into the mainstream, edwards' Joan story puts language itself on trial, questioning words' rigidity and disrupting language patterns to show what's possible.

One of the documents in edwards' archive in the SUNY Buffalo's Poetry Collection includes notes about her Joan of Arc project, an "artist statement" and "PROPOSED PROJECT,"[3] in which she outlines her plan for completing *dôNrm´-lä-püsl*, as well as a "PROPOSED BUGET."[4] In the notes attached to these documents, edwards writes that what first attracted her

---

3   kari edwards, "PROPOSED PROJECT" (Box 7, PCMS-40, kari edwards Collection, The Poetry Collection of the University Libraries, University at Buffalo, State University of New York, Buffalo, NY).

4   kari edwards, "PROPOSED BUGET." Unless otherwise noted, I preserve edwards' original spelling throughout this introduction.

to Joan's story was "exploring my linage." Her notes continue, "the disruption of gender, burnt at the stack for wearing men's cloths." At the end, she explains that even though Joan has been used throughout history for everything "from a nationaliist figure, procatholic figure, to a figure for womens rights and transgender rights," as edwards continued to learn more about Joan, she was touched by "how this person lived for the most part in a state of grace, a state of pure rapture and alignment with the universe, *living with the language of the heavens and wondering how could one speak of rapture*" (italics mine). It is not clear if the wondering edwards brings up here is her own wondering or Joan's; in either case, as is true throughout edwards' work, there is a clear emphasis on the importance of language. Tellingly, even though in the "PROPOSED PROJECT" she titles the manuscript *dôNrm ́-lä-püsl*, at the end of her notes she writes, "the title. beyond language." This shows that her focus with this project was on something that edwards in her "artist statement" calls "inadequacys of language," especially when it comes to gender. Where language fails, edwards' poetry enters.

The only record of Joan's story that is actually told from her perspective comes from the transcripts of her trial. In *Joan of Arc in Her Own Words,* Willard Trask gives us Joan's story, translated from the trial transcripts in French and arranged chronologically.[5] In a little over one hundred pages, we get an insight to Joan's mind — her resolve, quick wit, and sense of humor. But because we only get her lines, a lot of the context is missing and open to interpretation. Not surprisingly, most of the authors portraying Joan's story provide this context by

---

5   Willard Trask, *Joan of Arc in Her Own Words* (New York: Turtle Point, 1996).

appropriating Joan for their own purposes.[6] Bertolt Brecht's "Joan Dark,"[7] for example, is a Marxist Joan — a sort of missionary activist for the meatpacking workers in twentieth-century Chicago; Mark Twain's Joan[8] is the ideal Romantic heroine with all the saint-like virtues that a woman should possess; Vita Sackville-West's biography[9] underscores Joan's androgynous characteristics; and so on. These and other authors who write about Joan of Arc do give Joan a voice, but that voice is filtered through their own perceptions.

There have been too many Joan of Arc retellings to be able to discuss them all in this introduction,[10] so I will only mention a couple as an example of how Joan's story is deployed and appropriated. Like edwards, other authors put Joan of Arc in the context of their time and place, and endow Joan with characteristics they find important and which serve their own purposes. In "Joan of Arc Internationale: Shaw, Brecht, and the Law of Nations,"[11] Julie Stone Peters argues that Brecht was one of the first writers who focused on the whole legal system as the main culprit for Joan's death and disgrace:

---

6   Ann W. Astell discusses some of these retellings in her book (see footnote 2). Her focus in discussing these stories is on the concept of authorship — the relationships between Joan's story and the authors of her story. She also points out that the transcripts of Joan's trials are not only the first book about Joan, but also, she argues, the first one by her.

7   Bertolt Brecht, *Saint Joan of the Stockyards* (New York: Arcade, 1998).

8   Mark Twain, *Joan of Arc* (San Francisco: Ignatius, 1989).

9   Vita Sackville-West, *Saint Joan of Arc* (New York: Grove, 2001).

10 One useful resource that overviews depictions of Joan of Arc in literature since the middle ages is Ingvald Raknem's *Joan of Arc in History, Legend and Literature* (Oslo: Universitetsforlaget, 1971).

11 Julie Stone Peters, "Joan of Arc Internationale: Shaw, Brecht, and the Law of Nations" *Comparative Drama* 38.4 (2004–05): 355–77.

To attack only the "illegalities" of the trial, as so many others had done, would have been to suggest that the legal system itself was not at fault, but merely plagued by corrupt and malevolent judges. To attack directly the laws of the Inquisition would have been to attack a historical relic, to suggest, as so many others had, that a world made safe for democracy would now be safe for its saints and saviors. Both Shaw and Brecht were attempting, through their refigurations of the Joan of Arc myth, more fundamental critiques of the legal system itself, both national and international. (358)

Bertolt Brecht's Joan Dark (as he names the heroine of *Saint Joan of the Stockyards*) shares his anti-capitalist leanings. She helps the meatpacker workers through a group called Black Straw Hats:

> The workers' destinies are ruled by the coterie of owners (in fierce competition with one another), by the wild fluctuations of the stock market, which often result in massive layoffs and wage decreases, and by invisible forces in New York, which are mysteriously controlling international trade treaties. When the workers try to strike, the sentimental Pierpont Mauler, who weeps over the plight of the mooing cows on their way to the slaughter and swears to give up his murderous occupation, calls in the army, which brings in its tanks and machine guns, firing into the crowd, just as Brecht had seen the German police do at a communist rally in Berlin in the year he wrote *Die heilige Johanna*. (Stone Peters 365)

In Brecht's play, Joan and her group are tricked into actually helping the oppressor instead of the oppressed, and Brecht shows us how one person is not enough to institute any meaningful change. In this sense, Brecht uses Joan's story to put forward his beliefs. He does the same thing with two other Joan of Arc plays he wrote after this one.[12]

Similarly, Vita Sackville-West describes a Joan who in many respects resembles the author who is telling her story. In her essay on Sackville-West's biography of Joan, Karyn Z. Sproles writes, "Sackville-West does, I believe, idealize Joan of Arc — not as a saint or a visionary, but as an active woman who led the life of a man without becoming male" (158).[13] She talks about West's cross-dressing as one of the catalysts for her identification with Joan. But she also acknowledges the main difference — West cross-dressed to pass; Joan wore armor not to become a man — her transformation was "powerfully enabling, not transformative" (159).

Some of the most important markers of gender identity, and, particularly in Joan's case, rigid gatekeepers of gender norms and rules, are clothes. Interestingly, one of the original quotations that edwards uses in her manuscript, *"for you will not do what you say against me without suffering for it both in body and soul,"* is preceded in Trask's *Joan of Arc in Her Own*

---

12 After *Saint Joan of the Stockyards*, Brecht wrote two more Joan of Arc plays: *The Trial of Joan of Arc at Rouen 1431* (*Brecht: Collected Plays: Volume 9*, ed. Ralph Manheim and John Willet [New York: Pantheon, 1972], 147–88), in which he "interspersed material from the actual trial with commentary by French onlookers in order to address simultaneously (if only implicitly) both the questionable socialism of 'National Socialism' and the questionable legality of the Third Reich" and *The Visions of Simone Machard* (*Brecht: Collected Plays: Volume 7*, ed. John Willet and Ralph Manheim [New York: Bloomsbury, 1976], 1–65), "his third Joan of Arc play, written in collaboration with Lion Feuchtwanger in 1942–43, in response to the occupation of France" (Stone Peters 369–70).

13 Karyn Z. Sproles, "Cross-Dressing for (Imaginary) Battle: Vita Sackville-West's Biography of Joan of Arc," *Biography* 19. (1996): 158–77.

Words with, "When I shall have done that for which I am sent from God, I will put on women's clothing" (130). Joan says this in response to prosecutors asking her if she does not consider "our holy father the Pope" her judge. Her answer tells them that only when she completes her mission will she stop wearing men's clothing. In her mind, then, the clothes are connected to the character she is supposed to play. It also shows her resolve and tenacity, and, ultimately, her belief in God who (through the voices she has been hearing) guides her on the only possible path.

For edwards' Joan, clothes are a matter of practicality. In the following passage, for example, la pucelle talks about her choice of clothing, and though her choices at first allude to the feminine character (what a bride is supposed to wear on her wedding day), she quickly adds that the comfort of good boots is more important: "I decide between a red coat or metal leggings, maybe just borrowed, loaned, and or something blue. *though good boots always seem more useful than preconceived contrasts*" (italics mine). Clothes are also important during Joan's first meeting with her companion choisy: "from my first day here this giant glamor queen[14] approached me, or maybe it was the universe that brought us together. there huddled under the entry way to the universe with the smooth glow of dawn, dressed like one who could have been held in high regard in the medical profession but chose professional tennis as an option." We find out here that choisy is glamorous, but edwards also points out another important service of clothes — they can denote one's rank and profession. edwards' playfulness here also indicates the randomness of many possible

---

14 "Glamour queen" could be an allusion to drag queen, so edwards is hinting here already at choisy's gender fluidity.

interpretations of people's clothing choices. When choisy later asks la pucelle, "what of what you wear, red, maybe a little too much for nationalist testers and meeting off-shoot royals?" she responds, "I wear not what is expected, I wear for the indication, it's a matter of what suits me any more than that and it's too much sugar in the cake. there is work to be done here." For la pucelle, then, the clothes are her personal choice, and her point that "there is work to be done here" indicates that she does not want to spend much time discussing her sartorial choices.[15]

edwards' retelling is centered around Joan as a symbol of breaking gender barriers, but her Joan is also a fighter against rigid language norms. The pressing issues of language norms and oppression against the transgender body are what make edwards' intentionally anachronistic reinterpretation of the Joan of Arc story (with its direct application to current events) so important. la pucelle is a fighter for all those who are asked, as she writes, to "lie on their gender exam"[16] or to claim one normative gender. At the beginning of the manuscript, we meet Joan in a meditative state, not even sure where she is: "I could be somewhere else right now imagining being

---

15 The other possible reading would be that the clothes she is wearing help her get the work done.

16 From edwards' "Narrative/Identity":
> I mean, here I am riding along in my car and the gender police pull me over and demand that I circle either the, "F" or "M," and if don't, I am informed I won't receive my pension, subscription, monthly medication, food stamps, taxes, or student loan repayment plan. . . . and you know I have to laugh since I know, and you know, this gender thing is all made up, I know I was never a boy, and I know I was never a girl, so hey . . . where does that leave me . . . lying on my gender exam . . . so if I am lying . . . I want to know who else lies on the gender exam . . . go ahead raise your hands . . . it's fine, the destabilization process has already started . . .

here, imagining being somewhere else." However, edwards quickly moves on to situate us in the stark reality: "the verdict is in . . . they stack the wood . . . *I saw the fire lighted, the faggots are catching and the executioner . . . build(s) up the fire further . . .*" (original italics). Since we all know how Joan's life will end, it is an interesting choice for edwards to allude to Joan's death so early in the manuscript. It is a premonition and a reminder that despite the heroism of la pucelle, her story will and must end. This also indicates another type of awareness on edwards' part — that all of these retellings of Joan's story do not only confirm her heroism and martyrdom, but also participate in reliving Joan's death. Joan is symbolically killed — we kill her, as readers and writers, over and over again. In the words of la pucelle, "in these moments when I can catch my breath . . . these perfect pauses before being submerged again in the anguish of a billion torturous shrouds . . . *before I die again and again and again*" (italics mine). "*I saw the fire lighted, the faggots are catching and the executioner . . . builds up the fire further*" is also the first example of edwards using Joan's own (translated) words in her manuscript. The words in italics are Joan of Arc's words from her trial on Wednesday, May 23, 1431: "If I were at the place of execution, and I saw the fire lighted, and the fagots catching and the executioner ready to build up the tire, and if I were in the tire, even so I would say nothing else, and I would maintain what I have said at this trial until death. I have nothing more to say" (Trask 131–32). Joan is responding here to being threatened with torture. Her words show her resolve to stay true to her story and her beliefs. They also show her courage and willingness to face death for her cause.

Throughout edwards' edited document, she does not cite her sources, but she does signal to the reader which words are not hers by putting them in italics. In edwards' "PROPOSED PROJECT" document, she notes,

> each section [of the manuscript] has selections from la pucelle's documented voice, along with facts of the life documented and recorded in numerous trials and retrials as a direct transmission of la pucelle. there are also cuts and past quotes and sections from: julian of norwich, mark twain, lawrence stein, james joyce, getrude stein, raymond roussel, virgina wolf, and others.

Significantly, edwards adds, "this incorporation of other writers in to this text makes this the history of avant garde as a way to keep the idea of language out of bounds." Her Joan of Arc story, then, is a pastiche and a collection of different voices.[17] So, as edwards uses "sometimes, something, whatever, or both" in *a day in the life of p.* instead of pronouns "he" or "she," edwards uses other writers' (and Joan's own) words to get her message across.[18] These appropriations are more common in the first part of the document; later, for the most part, edwards' own words take over.

edwards uses Joan's words quite a few times in the manuscript, and those familiar with Joan's story would probably be able to recognize them even if they were not marked in italics. "*I would rather die than do what I know to be a sin,*" for example, are the words Joan utters after the siege of Orléans; she

---

17 Considering that Joan of Arc was guided by the voices of saints, perhaps with this appropriation of words by other writers edwards is guiding her la pucelle in a similar fashion.

18 kari edwards, *a day in the life of p* (New York: Subpress Collective, 2002).

is wounded, and when someone offers to charm her wounds, she responds with those words. Also, for example, after Joan revokes her abjuration, she says, "If I should say that God had not sent me, I should damn myself. It is true that God has sent me" (Trusk 140); edwards' Joan at one point exclaims, "*if I should say that heavens had not sent me I should damn myself.*" edwards adds, "*and then without warning long tumultuous shouting sounds like the voice of a thousand waters*," which is the last sentence from Edgar Allan Poe's "The Fall of the House of Usher." There are also quotes from Julian of Norwich, such as "*red blood trickling down from under the crown, all hot, flowing freely and copiously, a living stream, just as it seemed to me that it was at the time when the crown of thorns was thrust down.*" General pop culture references also appear in the text — for example the quote from the science fiction film *The Day the Earth Stood Still* in the following lines: "this is the place where I begin and end, alpha-betaomega, *klaatu barata nikto.*" In the document prepared by edwards, it is safe to assume that the italicized text was taken from some other work. But in the original, handwritten manuscript, the line between edwards' words and those she borrows is blurrier, and it is often impossible to tell where her words end and other authors' begin. She sometimes acknowledges her sources in marginal notes, but most of the time the reader is left to herself to either pick up the intertextual reference or miss it entirely.[19] She also mixes genres (macabre fiction, religious vision, personal accounts, etc.) and gender (by using both female and male authors' words). Thus, edwards opens the Joan story to all of literary history, bringing writers, religious

---

19   In this edition, we have included notes following the text to alert the reader to edwards' quotes and references.

mystics, and other artistic fellow travelers as allies and witnesses in Joan's trial.

The original journey of Joan to meet the Dauphine is replaced in edwards' version with la pucelle, a modern-day heroine, a gender warrior who travels long distances to meet "the one who knows" and to convince him that her fight is worth fighting. She doesn't make her journey riding on a horse; she takes "the local," with its cheap plastic seats and humming fluorescent lights, "to domrémy and beyond." [20] Joan's journey to get an audience with "the one who knows" is also repeated time and time again (she is continuously asked to go back and, just like the historical Joan of Arc, to return the next day for more questioning). This perhaps symbolizes not only Joan's long struggle to get an audience with the dauphin (and later her trial), but also the constant interrogation faced by people who don't strictly adhere to socially accepted gender rules and norms. la pucelle is thus someone who stands up for outcasts. She gives voice to those who might not have the courage to stand up and speak for themselves. She might not have a whole army to back her up, but she does have two companions by her side — "choisy" and "caeneus."

edwards' choice for Joan's companions is interesting, and it also stresses the importance of gender fluidity and freedom that she associates with Joan. The choice of "caeneus" is particularly telling: Caeneus is a character in Ovid's *Metamorphoses*. After Nestor briefly mentions Caeneus as one of the greatest warriors he has known and that he was born a woman, Achilles urges him to tell his whole story. Nestor obliges and tells the

---

20 Domrémy is the original name of Joan of Arc's birth village. It is now called Domrémy-la-Pucelle.

story of how Caenis who was famous for her beauty, is transformed into a great warrior Caeneus:

> But Caenis accepted none of her suitors.
> One day she was strolling along a secluded beach on her own,
> when, according to rumour's report, she was raped by the god of the sea.
> As Neptune savoured the joy of his latest conquest, he said,
> "I'll allow you to ask for a gift which I promise not to refuse you.
> Now choose what you want to ask me!" (so the rumour continued)
> Caenis replied: "The wrong you have done me is great, so I'll ask you
> the greatest of favours I can: let me never be able to suffer
> such wrong again. If you will make me a woman no more,
> your promise will be fulfilled." She delivered those final words
> in a lower voice, and they might have appeared to come from a man —
> as they surely did. The god of the sea has already granted
> Caenis' request and had also bestowed an additional power:
> the new male body can never be wounded or fall at a sword's point. (473–74)[21]

edwards would have been attracted to this story because it involves transformation and triumph; from the aftermath of

---

21   Ovid, *The Metamorphoses,* trans. David Raeburn (New York: Penguin, 2004).

gender-based violence change and growth is possible — a great warrior can emerge.

Joan's other companion, "choisy" is modeled after François-Timoléon de Choisy (1644–1724), a transvestite French writer and abbot. Nancy Arenberg writes,

> From a young age, Choisy's mother, seeking to further her social ambitions in the court, dressed her son as a girl in the hopes of cultivating the friendship of the King's brother. She succeeded in her plan since Choisy was a frequent visitor to the court; he soon became the playmate of Philippe d'Orléans. Their mutual fondness for feminine fashion, jewelry, make-up and other accessories was never concealed at court. In fact, Philippe's travesty of gender was even encouraged, since it would diminish any threat to Louis' absolute power. Choisy's growing taste for women's clothes did not, however, disappear as he grew up and became a man. During the course of his life, he alternated between periods of cross-dressing and reverting to his masculine clothing, and more often than not to his ecclesiastic robes. (13–14)[22]

Arenberg's description of Choisy is suggestive of edwards' interest in this sexually ambiguous figure. Choisy's connection to French court and princely power must have proven irresistible to one approaching the topic of Joan-as-gender-warrior, and the idea of "alternating" freely between gender identities would certainly have been appealing as well. Paul Scott, however, contends that Choisy's memoirs of dressing as a woman

---

22 Nancy Arenberg, "Mirrors: Crossdressing and Narcissism in Choisy's *Histoire de Madame la Comtesse de Barres*," *Cahiers du dix-septième* X.1 (2005): 11–30.

are a complete fabrication: "the inescapable conclusion is that they represent nothing other than an elaborate and sustained fantasy on their creator's part."[23] Scott points to a lack of "supporting evidence," or any mention of Choisy's cross-dressing by any of his contemporaries. Whether edwards supposed Choisy to be fabricating the account is, in some sense, irrelevant (and there is every indication edwards took it at face value); yet edwards might have found the idea of Choisy's faked gender-bending to accord well with her sense that gender is fluid and ever-changing.

This gender-bending is amplified by edwards' decision to take some of the lines she gives to choisy directly from Chevalier d'Eon, another interesting eighteenth-century gender-bending figure. d'Eon's story is particularly fascinating because during his lifetime it was largely thought that he was born a woman and lived as man in order to be able to rise publicly; the truth, however, was the other way around. As Gary Kates writes,

> During the last decade of the Old Regime the Chevalière d'Eon was considered one of the most famous and accomplished women of the eighteenth century. After all, no other woman of the Chevalière's age had achieved what d'Eon had: become a major diplomat who negotiated the 1763 Treaty of Paris with England; a military hero who was awarded the highly coveted Cross of Saint Lois for military valor; and an author of over fifteen volumes, mostly on government finance.

---

23 Paul Scott, "Authenticity and Textual Transvestism in the Memoirs of the Abbé de Choisy," *French Studies: A Quarterly Review* 69.1 (2015): 14–29.

> What fascinated European commentators was that all of this had been achieved by not only a woman but by a woman who has also posed as a man. . . .
>
> When d'Eon finally died in 1810, everyone, including Mrs. Cole, d'Eon's housemate of fifteen years, was shocked to discover the naked truth: the eighty-one-year-old chevalière actually possessed a male body, ordinary in every way. (558–59, 561)[24]

Thus, edwards' interest in d'Eon is not surprising, and her choice to create a character who is a mixture of Choisy and d'Eon shows her desire to weave the history of transgender lineage into her work, as well as, again, point out the fluidity of any kind of identity, but especially that of gender.[25]

Like many of edwards' other works, this manuscript is also unconventional when it comes to narrative techniques — it is not linear in terms of time and space, and it is not binary when it comes to gender.[26] For example, throughout the text edwards keeps destabilizing the idea of time and reminding the readers that Joan does not fully belong to the past, just as she does not fully belong to the present. When she talks about

---

24 Gary Kates, "The Transgendered World of the Chevalier/Chevalière d'Eon," *The Journal of Modern History* 67.3 (1995): 558–94.

25 For more on d'Eon see Charles d'Eon de Beaumont, *The Maiden of Tonnerre: The Vicissitudes of the Chevalier and the Chevalière d'Eon*, trans. Roland A. Champagne, Nina Claire Ekstein, and Gary Kates (Baltimore: The Johns Hopkins University Press, 2004).

26 In fact, in her "PROPOSED PROJECT," edwards explains that everything happens in a span of a single day, "the text is broken into seven parts, from prevision (or darkness) to light (or after death). it moves through the day, from nighttime to high noon when the 'la pucelle' was actually burnt at the stake."

being tortured, la pucelle wonders if her remains will be "scattered on the future sight of a 7–11." When Joan describes her long and repeated journey to "the one who knows," edwards also sprinkles several current concepts into this paragraph:

> *I ride the local* everyday, or I attempt to take it every day and every day it's the same thing. I arrive, *I mind the gap* and take a seat. I look across from me and see the person to the right is the same person. maybe this is a visionaries' waiting room, yet, every day as before, tests, exams, questions of my whereabouts on this day and that day. who spoke to me and have I ever left my *carry on luggage* anywhere. (italics mine)

Later in the manuscript, there is also mention of a "tupperware container," and the notion that Joan's message should be delivered "through the post office overnight express," and so on. The mention of such anachronistic objects and concepts breaks the narrative temporally, introducing a diachronic element that connects us with Joan and makes her story more immediate. These objects and concepts also converse with edwards' ideas about gender — that it is fluid; that it involves movement and gaps; that there are "containers" that we are put in and must break out of. There is even one occasion when edwards uses Joan to ventriloquize a kind of meta-commentary on this work. When Joan is trying to get an audience with "the one who knows," she tells her interrogators to tell him that "that was the universe straightening out the sheets, not some probate indication writing up so called historical fictional characterizations." But what is the meta-commentary edwards is making? The word "probate" can be a noun, a verb, or an adjective, and thus it fits with edwards' idea of nouns becoming verbs. "Probate" is also (mostly) a legal term; a probate court has jurisdiction over matters relating to wills. The word is derived from Latin "probare," which means "to prove."[27] Thus Joan's commentary mocks the jurisdiction of her interrogators, asserting the supremacy of "the universe" or perhaps edwards' own writing.

The Joan of Arc project is a continuation of edwards' playing with language: throughout the manuscript, edwards alludes to how language affirms norms and, at the same time, is inadequate in its possibilities to express something as nuanced and layered as gender. And though the original Joan was fighting for her country and her king, la pucelle, "dress[ed] in armor that caeneus offered, shinning and ready to do battle with proverbs and pronouns," has a different fight in mind. edwards had previously engaged in this "battle with proverbs and pronouns" in *a day in the life of p.*, and she also addresses it more in her unpublished essay "The Voices of Ten Thousand Genders: A Inquiry Into One Hundred Years of Alternative Gender Literature." edwards outlines the goals of this essay as follows,

> In examining alternative gendered writings I hope to bring some continuity to the history of a group of people that has been, until recently, fragmented, adapted, obliterated or assimilated. I also intend to show that these texts constitute a persistent alternative to the master narratives of gender, a counter-discourse. I will focus on the language of resistance used even at times when resistance of the dominant culture was followed by the swift response of "the law." This is the language of individuals

---

27   "probate, n." *OED Online*. Oxford University Press, December 2015. Web.

who have written themselves into existence despite a lack of language to adequately represent them.

Here, language of resistance has two meanings: it is that which dares to be spoken, but it is also language that is, just like in edwards' *a day in the life of p.*, pliable. It is also the language that needed to be invented by those who until they invented it could not speak of their experiences. Discussing language that is flexible and adjustable in the same way as gender, edwards chooses to rebel against the artificial stability of either of these two concepts. She writes,

> When bodies become malleable so does language. When primary sexual indicators no longer locate the gender of that individual, the signifying economy is disrupted. Language loses it[s] function to signify, pronouns no longer have viability, or become. As C. Jacob Hale states, we "are living in a historical discursive moment in which our language has run out" (1997, p. 335).[28] Alternative gendered individuals' presence, and their literature, are bringing language as we know it to a point where it must expand to encompass the not yet readable. This is the historical struggle against ideological fixation, "the struggle against the codes that translate all meaning perfectly" (Haraway, 1991, p.176).[29]

---

28 Jacob C. Hale, "Consuming the Living, Dis(re)membering the Dead in the Butch/Ftm Borderlands," *Journal of Lesbian and Gay Studies:* 4.2 (1998): 311–38.

29 Donna Haraway, *Simians, Cyborgs, and Women: The Reinvention of Nature* (New York: Routledge, 1991).

These passages from "The Voices of Ten Thousand Genders" encapsulate edwards' main stance on gender and language. Unlike *a day in the life of p.*, the Joan of Arc manuscript does not directly interrupt established language codes by inventing new words, but edwards constantly stresses that one of the fights Joan is fighting is related to gender and language.

The importance of language for edwards in this project is evident from its title. According to her notes, she at first proposes *Beyond Language*, but then she chooses the title *dôNrm-lä-püsl*, an approximation of a phonetic transcription of Domrémy-la-Pucelle, Joan's birth village. From a quick visual scan, the reader can at once sense edwards' effort to connect to the non-normative, to the unspeakable, by virtue of our inability to say the title's name and the discomfort that goes along with this inability. We might detect the word "norm" in "dôNrm" and, perhaps, the message "do" or "do not norm," and in a similar way, one could read the name of Joan's companion choisy as a pun on "choice."

edwards' idea of "language out of bounds" is expressed in several places in the manuscript. When la pucelle describes one tool of torture ("this rusted rake being drawn across my skin") as "nothing more than a ragged sentence that has fallen out off the page — lifeless carcass telling lies," edwards seems to indicate that the meaning, and thus truthfulness, of language (a "ragged sentence") in or outside the text, is not to be taken for granted. When Joan talks about her vision at the beginning of the second section, she also refers to language existing not only in the text itself, but also outside of it. Joan, guided by the light, is looking for "a seat on a the local to cross the boundary of the page." This light is also referred to as "a sermon without words." During one of her questionings, Joan says, "I have been sent in part to bring zero language." And when she is talking to choisy for the first time, she says, "but soon we will see places change from things to verbs. it will be miraculous, but I think you already know that and know what to do." In another instance, edwards explicitly points out that the problem is the rigidity of nouns (which, compared to verbs, are stable): "on the field of grass of grain of pleasure, on the field of yesteryear tomorrow and the next one to come, on the field bloodied with too many nouns." And soon after, "after the night has settled and gone away. after the morning light had been readjusted. after dressing in armor that caeneus offered, shinning and ready to do battle with proverbs and pronouns." All these examples speak to edwards' insistence on how language, just like gender, should be flexible, pliable, and not complicit in policing the strictness of the gender binary.

The mention of "zero writing" also echoes Roland Barthes' *Writing Degree Zero*, and Joan is perhaps an avatar for edwards' desire to approach the "zero degree, pregnant with all past and future specifications."[30] But as always with edwards, even this desire is not so straightforward. Barthes continues, "[e]ach poetic word is thus an unexpected object, a Pandora's box from which fly out all the potentialities of language" (48). So far, so good; and edwards would seem to strongly agree with the idea of unleashing "all the potentialities of language," especially if that means freeing the self from gender binaries. But: "This Hunger of the Word, common to the whole of modern poetry, makes poetic speech terrible and inhuman" (48). "Terrible" because, as Barthes adds, "there is no humanism of modern poetry. This erect discourse is full of terror, that is to say, it relates man not to other men, but to the most inhuman images in Nature: heaven, hell, holiness, childhood, madness,

---

30 Roland Barthes, *Writing Degree Zero*, trans. Annette Lavers and Colin Smith (New York: Hill and Wang, 1967).

pure matter, etc." (50). Yet "thing" language, the word as pure object, does not seem to be what edwards is after; in a sense we observe edwards approach "zero" only to, at the last moment, add rather than subtract possibilities — and precisely on the plane of embodied humanity. Take, for example, the mention above of Joan "ready to do battle with proverbs and pronouns." On the one hand, we imagine Joan contending *against* proverbs and pronouns, especially those that would tend to impose and box in gender. On the other, are we not also invited to imagine Joan fighting *with, along side of,* proverbs and pronouns? This second sense of the phrase gains credence if we recall edwards' inventive, experimental, potential-laden use of pronoun substitutes in *a day in the life of p.*

edwards' la pucelle is not only a fighter for her country and "heavens," but through telling her story edwards is able to connect the text to a contemporary way of discussing embedded gender constraints. la pucelle is also aware of these constraints and fights against them. When she meets choisy for the first time, choisy tells her, "I've heard rumor of you and that you're here to remove the veil, I would like to serve with you in the struggle, since I am also from a place of boxes box cutter, which usually fit horribly, and bleed heavily." The veil choisy refers to is, seemingly, the blindness of those who choose not to see beyond the aforementioned gender norms. The boxes here can be metaphorical boxes one is supposed to fit in perfectly and never think outside of them; but they can also stand for literal boxes, the ones that require us to check one or the other to indicate "male" or "female." choisy's words here show solidarity with Joan, who also doesn't fit neatly into either of these categories, and it also alludes to the violence perpetuated against those who don't fit. If one does not fit in a box, "the box cutter" is going to be used to make them fit. Soon after choisy joins her, la pucelle is hopeful that she can, indeed, bring about change: "I knew after that brief moment I was on my way to turning this around, I also knew they would try to find a box for both of us to fill out, but I know if I could connive those inquisitors I could finally throw these boxes out." She is aware that she and choisy will be forced to fit in, but she is also positive that she can overthrow this kind of thinking and get rid of such attempts. She later tells her inquisitors, "I have come to give a sign to the one who knows, I have come to help raise a siege against those forces that grasp labels with bloodied stumps just to receive their months' disablement checks." The siege "la pucelle" refers to is not the famous siege of Orléans that Joan raised in 1429; it is the siege that forces certain labels on people. What edwards also acknowledges is that this siege is futile and that both those who fight to maintain it and those on the other side get hurt. Further, those maintaining the siege do so not because they necessarily believe in its mission, but because they can benefit from it. Such is edwards' commentary on any belief systems that establish artificial hierarchies and rules in order to maintain power. Her Joan, then, is a heroine who will help to overhaul the system, but, as she says, "I am here to show us set us there and there but I can't do it on my own."

When Joan finally puts on armor, it makes her feel like "a mythical figure born in the castration of the sea. I was ready, we were ready, ready to take the domrémy line to new sovereign and beyond to begin again." It is this readiness for the new beginning, for taking up the journey and the fight yet again (at least in this first section of the manuscript), that makes edwards' Joan relevant and important because it gives us, like the original Joan and those who followed, hope that a better world, one without restrictive boxes and violent box cutters, is possible. It also tells us that we should demand it for ourselves.

Working on *dôNrm´-lä-püsl* was exciting and terrifying at the same time. Exciting because I was privileged to be one of the first — if not the first — people reading edwards' unpublished work. Terrifying because there was great pressure on my editorial efforts and whether they could do the work justice. No matter how carefully and meticulously I approached the manuscript, I knew that it was impossible to shape the work exactly as edwards would have wanted it.

My first archival discoveries were the notebooks with the handwritten manuscript of the Joan of Arc project. However, I also found a typewritten draft of the first part of the project in one of the boxes. When I contacted Frances Blau about editing and publishing this already typed-up document, she was delighted and surprised. She did not know that edwards had formalized any portion of this work.[31] So even though I spent quite some time transcribing the handwritten notebooks, this text reflects my edited version of the document edwards typed up herself.[32] Next to this document, edwards filed the "PROPOSED PROJECT,"[33] in which she discusses how she envisions this project, but also mentions her dyslexia and her need for editorial guidance. She writes, "I am severely dyslexic and the assistance of an editor is of the utmost importance, for without one I have to rely on friends and loved

---

31   edwards did, however, post a part of this project on her blog: http://transdada.blogspot.com/2003/10/from-dnrm-l-psl-prelude-this-could-be.html

32   I am hoping to return to the handwritten notebooks in the future.

33   Though there is no address or other record that would indicate to whom and where edwards sent or planned on sending this manuscript, the existence of the typed pages together with this proposal can be seen as proof that she was planning on finding a publisher for this project, or that she was seeking financial support for it in a form of a fellowship of some kind.

ones." When I worked on the notebooks, edwards' dyslexia and her scrawling penmanship made movement through the manuscript exceptionally difficult: it was nearly impossible at times to decipher the words on the page. But I do not regret that labor; on the contrary. The fact that I transcribed some pages from those notebooks and was later able to see edwards' own transcript was helpful: it not only gave me useful insights into her editing process, but it also helped me make decisions when I set out to edit her typewritten pages.

Even though working with the typed manuscript was much easier than working with the handwritten notebooks, there was still a good amount of editorial work required. There were some parts in which it seemed pretty clear what edwards was trying to say; most pages, however, took a lot of time and more deliberating about what edwards intended. Likewise, some of the words in the manuscript were more easily deciphered than others. I knew that when edwards writes in the proposal that la pucelle was "burnt at the stack," she means "stake." Also, "clearing sound of chiken moans and pit bowls" was revised to "clearing sound of chicken moans and pit bulls" without much difficulty. Sometimes, however, it took weeks to decide on a single word or phrase. And even after the decision was made, I would go back to a certain word and phrase after reading through the manuscript again and change it to something else, something I thought worked better or made more sense.

One of the most involved and in the end the most rewarding processes was trying to pin down who la pucelle's companions are. edwards spells "choisy" and "caenus" several different ways throughout the manuscript: "chosy," "chosisy," "choisy," "chosiy," "chaosy," "chsy," "caenis," "canus," "cans," "canous," "cnaus."[34] I at first thought that "choisy" was edwards' pun on the word "choice." This explanation fits well with edwards' position on the fluidity and choice of one's gender and gender expression. Likewise, there are instances in the text that suggested that "choisy" could in fact be either a woman or a man. As it turned out, my explanation was partially correct, but in fact referred, as I discovered after some research, to François-Timoléon de Choisy, as described previously.

In other instances where it was difficult for me to work out a word or a phrase due to spelling, I had to eventually make a best-guess decision. This was a task that I had the most difficulty doing, as I understand that one word can make all the difference in how a text is read. I also realize that a different reader might have chosen a different word. And neither one of us might be "correct," since edwards' intention could be entirely different.

Here are a few examples of what the original pages looked like, followed by my editorial revisions:

> "weaving stright at me from the grande quzine of comnamd in guttraal retention"

> "first the first things first we must know of local peteiclars so first things first?"

> "I am sent here to stiop the atrocities before its to late. sex or not has not barring on the wheather. all you need

---

34 These different spellings are listed here in the order of their appearance in the manuscript.

to know is I am more than suritable to show secrets of an ever expanive soul."

In my version, these lines read:

"waving straight at me from the grand cuisine of command in guttural retention"

"first the first things first we must know of local practitioner so first thing's first?"

"I am sent here to stop the atrocities before it's too late. sex or not has no bearing on the weather. all you need to know is I am more than suitable to show secrets of an ever expansive soul."

As one can see, some of the words, such as "suritable," for example, are simple misspellings; others took more deliberation and thinking. In the above selections, the most difficult for me to decide on was "local practitioner." edwards' "peteiclars" reminded me of French dessert "petite éclairs," which would disrupt the meaning of the sentence in a fun way and give it a local peculiarity. There was also a possibility of "local particulars." In the end, local practitioner made the most sense, since this figure comes up a few times later in the manuscript, and it became clear that it is a reference to the priest from Joan's village.

Some might, of course, ask: why not just leave edwards' spelling as is? After all, especially in this case, for example, her (mis)spellings invite one to imagine all the possibilities I mention (and, of course, most likely many more). In a few cases in the manuscript, I actually did leave edwards' spelling untouched. However, since the work that follows is my own edition of the text, I had to make certain decisions. Leaving everything as is would defeat the purpose of editing the manuscript, and the original is available in the SUNY Buffalo's Poetry Collection. Likewise, as is clear from Frances Blau's description of edwards' editorial process, this manuscript would not be considered finished by edwards herself.[35] While making editorial decisions, I tried to strike a balance between my interpretations of edwards' words and the possibilities of other interpretations. I believe that given her project, which aims to show both the limitations and endless possibilities of language, this kind of approach was appropriate.

In the end, this book must be called a possible "version" of edwards' manuscript. I take full responsibility for my decisions, even as I acknowledge that what follows surely would not have been the final version of *dôNrm´-lä-püsl* if edwards had lived to see it through to publication. In every writer's archive there are previously unread and undiscovered manuscripts. There are notes, letters, and unfinished projects, and increasingly, as is the case with edwards, electronic materials, word files, emails, blog posts. . . . Many of these items are best left to the specialist or the scholar who might, reading them, gain a better understanding of the author's extant work. Previously unpublished work is unpublished for a reason, and is often better left that way. My discovery of edwards' Joan of Arc project, however, is different. Not only did edwards clearly intend for this work to be published — as the copious plans, project and budget outlines attest — but also, as I have shown, the work provides an important, even essential, further extension of edwards' lifelong artistic and activist pursuits. In her

---

35 See Frances Blau's essay "My Words" in Julian T. Brolaski, erica kaufman, and E. Tracy Grinnell, ~~kari edwards~~: *NO GENDER: Reflections on the Life & Work of kari edwards* (Brooklyn: Belladonna/Litmus, 2009), 9–14.

Joan of Arc, edwards forges an exciting new direction in these pursuits, one that I was excited to discover in the notebooks and eager to bring to other readers. The Joan of Arc project, though incomplete, can be seen as culmination of her ongoing work and, on that merit alone, is a significant addition to edwards' visible poetics.

Tina Žigon

prelude

    emptiness and a new trauma. a new place, a new empty situation, not a penetrating one. maybe a car gently being pushed into the abyss, replaced by the terror of form disappearing and that typical panic. it could be the inevitable impact scream that never comes, preceding brake squeals, then nothing. it could be something else and this could be that something else, this could be a reminder, a message of something that may have occurred and I am only saying this is this and this is the darkness of the past that leaks through clipping sounds. there is no option "a," since there was never option "b."

    I could be somewhere else right now imagining being here, imagining being somewhere else. I suppose

I could be traveling on a highway just outside somewhere else, watching the thunder roll over a demoralized horizon, outside a captured territory demanding liberty for those past lives held in perpetuity. I could be speaking of solitude to my personal martyrs.

are you listening?

The random is on darkness . . . the verdict is in . . . they stack the wood . . . *I saw the fire lighted, the faggots are catching and the executioner . . . build(s) up the fire further* . . . hands won't show themselves. faces hide. the corners are ground down and obscure. sounds creep through with muffled ankles bound ever so tightly . . . is that roaches or the hum of an invasion. maybe, cement crumbling from years of memorized transgressions. it could be the day the earth stood still consuming itself in large evangelist chunks.

the only edge I know is this cold embankment that seeps dampness into skeletal remains . . . pulverizing muscles with the constant pull towards the core. so, I work another miracle that goes unrecorded, watch each cell destroy themselves, with neat military precision. one soldier after another cut down with steel blade projectiles in a napalm moment.

I know somewhere someone is working with someone to create the perfect offense, the inescapable question, the inscrutable nutcracker, the unexplainable iron maiden cause and effect . . . a joint venture . . . it could be patent pending . . . in the name of the queen/king, country . . . bless amerika and all that.

the pain creeps through pores . . . expanding along the inner layers of flesh, discharging urgent messages to my prefrontal context, assaulting the walls of my defenses, turning this body into nothing more than a dead zone of inarticulate tremors longing for immediate extraction.

I lay here . . . move from one dead zone to the next with only a second reprieve . . . a second when my breath is not chopped in half in a gangrenous scream . . . a moment when the terror stops in anticipation of termination . . . bit by bit . . . organ by organ . . . cell by cell . . . bringing everything to-a-close due to lack of recognition. *and there . . . from within and from without, by which we may know. I know well that I have deserved pain . . . and . . . punish me wisely. for you will not do what you say against me without suffering for it both in body and soul.*

in these moments when I can catch my breath . . . these perfect pauses before being submerged again in the anguish of a billion torturous shrouds . . . before I die again and again and again, there in the lesion that opens into a hallway to the lessons being given, chapter and verse *on the red blood trickling down from under the crown, all hot, flowing freely and copiously, a living stream, just as it seemed to me that it was at the time when the crown of thorns was thrust down.*

and then without warning *long tumultuous shouting sounds like the voice of a thousand waters* that slice a maniac's path along my tendons, my veins my muscles to announce the end of sanity.

a moment longer on the edge and my body voids itself — collapsing to nothing but an impermanent stain.

I rotate to a position not recovering from the previous one-dimensional felony.
I would rather die than do what I know to be a sin.

I catch my breath for an instant and focus on infinity, which counts more than gold and comes before and after repetition and ideology. how did I come to this moment of suffocation? who chose me? could it be that I am not here? could it be that this rusted rake being drawn across my skin is nothing more than a ragged sentence that has fallen off the page — a lifeless carcass telling lies.

it could be I have forgotten that *I could suffer more as a reminder of the four ways of passion . . . the bleeding of the head, . . . the discoloration of the flesh . . . copious bleeding of the body and deep dying.*

it could be I have missed the endless confession of my sins and now suffer the abandon of torturers who douse me in kerosene to manufacture language with lit cigarettes — or was after being horse raped by trained pedestrians looking for more glass to break, after arrows didn't produce the desired effect, hacked from limb-to-limb, scattered on the future sight of a 7-11.

I was asked if I was willing to repent and mend my ways.

if I should say the heavens had not sent me I should damn myself.

if I could see *the furrows which have made a bed for themselves in my colorless cheeks*, if I could perceive that which I can not name, that which crushes my body into a steel box or something significantly smaller than "a," compacting me into neat symmetrical order, all accomplished by chatty machines, constructed and assembled at their plant of origin, labeled, categorized, numbered and shipped to the appropriate equivalent.

how many numbers does it take to convince the near dead to lead or a child or something else?

I protest against being kept in these chains and irons.
I come, sent by the heavens. I have no business here.

the world turns and I weep. the body turns and I weep. the body clock rotates with a momentum casting itself as the enola gay, bathed in sins, rotating on a spit stuffed, hoof and mouth, bubbling surface flames, leaving no shadows, no glimmer, no reservation, just a language vortex or something else, producing a new floral nightmare, as the earth stiffens in the reflection of emerging discarded flesh parts.

if you were to have me torn limb from limb and sent my soul out of my body, I would say nothing else to satisfy your inquiry. *as for signs; if those who ask for them are not worthy of it, I am not accountable for that.*

this is all probably one of those dreams I will wake up in. one where the television set is on runaway and some savior is watching the blank screen. I know I have no choice but to listen and take off my red jacket, stop spinning and proceed . . . yes, it's true I had many godparents, two popes, and the voices, sweet with temple honey, voices I confess to, voices that tell me I am here.

what here? a left hand turn at a cheap hotel with rude jailers before my birth and after my death.

this is the place where I begin and end, alphabetaomega, *klaatu barata nikto.*

boning burns like artificial limbs, like pierced necks and backs with distinguishable lines protruding. like a dog without a bark. like friendly bombs.

the heat empties from the body, the after shock or a torn memory from a different perspective oozes blood from behind mental armor.

it could be something else and this could be that something else.

this pain, this darkness could be nothing more than a reminder that something happened, a tear something leaked through, carrying clicking or electrical or heavenly something.

I could be somewhere else imagining being here. outside a wall shouting

—I am sent by the heavens. *I do my best to serve.*

who has abandoned me to this darkness?
I don't know either a or b
I come from the kingdom of heaven to raise the siege and where am I now?
I was *so horribly and cruelly used*
that I damned myself to save my life.

hear my confession, my sins, all deeds against others . . . blood everywhere . . . caught in distorted bodies . . . too much to bear . . . to confess . . . I have orders to follow . . . *I die through you* . . . I have orders to follow . . . *even if it costs me my head* . . . *I have orders to follow* . . . *I ask for help from no one* . . . *I have come* . . . *I was sent by the heavens.*

2.

    in this vision I approach the light, everyone does.

    in this vision I always approach the light, as if it's not so much a light as a door that opens, so I can find a seat on the local to cross the boundary of the page.

    in this vision I approach the light, as does everyone else.

    in this vision I always approach the light as does the rest. it's not so much a light as the comforts of a fluorescent flicker on the local bathed in a sermon without words. I can hear it speak when the doors open, sitting on red plastic seats, as others who, always the same as if this is dream repeat, but it's not, I can tell by the smells on the local domrémy line to new sovereign and beyond.

always the aroma of stagnated urine from these endless battle lines — on this and every droning moan, this rocket red glare, "listening to the flicker that parachutes behind enemy lines. . . ."

this is why I preferred the fluorescent, it's always the same that gather, in the same position, in the same moment, one enters then pressed air hisses, closed doors, a jerk and we become destiny or pick more of those who are the same, arriving from every world, but the same from then and now here to then to take the domrémy line to new sovereign and beyond.

I decide between a red coat or metal leggings, maybe just borrowed, loaned, and or something blue. though good boots always seem more useful than preconceived contrasts. whether at the altar or loom, it takes one to know one, so it's better to be known than not vote with both hands on the wheel — even if you haven't got it yet, you will along with all the merchandizing effects.

it's always the same, I tear up the contract to the displeasure in a huff and puff of preconception, since I know that the flicker will lead to the end of the line.

the fluorescent is always softer than that false dawn requirements, doing KP duties for the home team, day in and day out. as someone said, sign here and it's yours for life. honestly, I could never see chicken giblets and canning as my way of life, especially after the difference of antigone's way. I would look elsewhere and a while, but even a flicker seems like a promise, especially when it spoke so low, so eternally low, dripped in honey tones, massaging ventral veins with deep calming reassurance, beyond a simple something, but I stood my ground as a conversation piece, a simple howdoyoudo and without notice I realized this was no stranger you find at a dinner sniffin' the ground down dregs and chewin' old hens, honest to real, there, surrounded by boundless affection held in the eternal hand, right there on a promise brighter than sight, listening to and basking in the hand that is the hand that is the hand and never was forever and more being told of a peaceful rebirthing projects and boundless horizons. and after passing the test, that was basically, sure why not since there was no true or false, just the ability to see criteria, we would all go and settle in a bed of fragrance carved out of newborn sucking milk. although the test was another matter for some not necessary, who choose to stay and continue the task without pay, cleaning infested lessons and repairing wounded routes of different times, for others it was as easy as one-two-three strike a match, there you are, presto — you're it, next. could it be that simple? I wanted to ask but it seemed like asking what came first a western or a denver omelet?

that was then and this is then and now and I must take my seat, the others have arrived as they always do. I never see them enter. they're just there. I suspect that until they take the domrémy line to new sovereign they go by different names and have different life times. but isn't that the way it is, you keep the home fires burning until one flicks the mumblety-peg, then you're it, and you can never go home again.

though I can never see them clearly since there are always nothing more than a comfortable lukewarm *comme ce comme ça*, just enough to make sure you're on the right parallelogram, just enough to see your hand before you fade. I can always tell it's them, maybe it's second nature, or some kind of cockpit voice recorder that's in the know now and then. I don't know what it is, but I know it's them, as if I have been coming here all my life and before that.

as always, as if for the first time the train jerks to motion and enters the tunnel disavowing any relaxation from street level, leaving a warm fluorescent halo that fails at each curve and each track connection casting doubt upon moments of darkness and lost histories.

and here we are at false dawn, the sudden instant after absolute darkness falls, we could be the survivors of a plane crash meeting for the first time, left over in formaldehyde dreams, but we are here and they are the faces that acknowledge the truthfulness of rocks, they have seen their own eyes face-to-face, laying in their blood as it comes into vision.

the lights flash on, then off, yanking one from another world to a red plastic seat, the same as before, the same as it always has been, there we sit looking at each other and not acknowledging each other and knowing any false glances could tear the hearts out of those that think they stand on bedrocks, that is really nothing more than a silly footed love song.

I ride the local everyday, or I attempt to take it every day and every day it's the same thing. I arrive, I mind the gap and take a seat. I look across from me and see the person to the right is the same person. maybe this is a visionaries' waiting room, yet, every day as before, tests, exams, questions of my whereabouts on this day and that day. who spoke to me and have I ever left my carry on luggage anywhere. every day they say come back, try again, they say could you repeat this vision or that vision describe in detail, step by step each iridescent taste of ecstasy. I keep saying,

—*I do not know a from b,* you must know I would *rather . . . sit and sew besides my poor* parents. so take your persecution truefalse am I on the scale yet in the safe part of the bell curve yet — *rather now than tomorrow, and tomorrow than the day after.*

only to be told, soon, soon at which I respond as always,

twice and thrice a week the voices told me that I must depart.

I buy my ticket on the domrémy local every day only to be told to return. return again tomorrow and tomorrow. my only solace is the faces I see as I take the red seat and the voices that tell me to take the domrémy line to new sovereign and beyond.

I keep telling them I must speak to the one who knows I had a vision and know how to relieve the segregation that has emptied the sailed air from our soul. I keep telling them I must speak to the one who knows that I see beyond the forms required to fill out initiation of an appropriated interview. don't deceive me I had a vision, I am here from a higher order. I am here to stop atrocity.

I had the will to believe in something different, something beyond the cheaply reproduced documents. I keep saying over and over — I ask for help from no one, I have come, I was sent by the universe, I have those who believe, those who take this endless line from domrémy to new sovereign with the help of the stars above. I stand against the bleeding beast suffocating boxed form, pelted with darkness and wrought with end of my own breath. I must proceed, I must make them see I will pass your silly test no matter where I come from is of no concern.

—but since you ask.

—we asked.

the voices always come from square edges adorned with gold mules and synthetic silk power beast of the holly collar. I come every day to the scale version of downed statuary flanked by flaying gas masked bayonets. every day I go to the internal investigation of the speculative whereabouts which so happens is right next door to the warehouse for the criminally insane. the lift never works so ten flights become my fluorescent dream time until the edged aroma of open sewers and the burning plagueish fear.

just beyond the door crouched the judas, tester, executioner, seven in all with a badger like center making clearing sound of chicken moans and pit bulls. seven, three adornments on each side of this grumbling center piece. replaying the — come in, come in come in we've heard so much and want to tell you what we know . . . every day it's the same line from different directions

—so please tell us what have others thought of all these visions, their version of your vision, can you give us a recipe, a letter of reference, a dialogue you recall, anything, high school transcripts?

—I would like to know about mutant fairies demons?

waving straight at me from the grand cuisine of command in guttural retention congested hog swallow followed with empty footsteps of the others who fall into situational cock sucking order.

—first the first things first we must know of local practitioner so first thing's first?

—do you herd the herd and how hard is it to help yourself there or there?

slipping over the lips from an echoed mind in a different onslaught.

—what of the visions, the visions what of the visions in color, black and white glossies and who stars in it. names, we must have names and address?

the grand inquisitor only grunted interruption or interrupted with grunts in this direction or that indicating with like a swallow bovine on automatic fly distraction mode.

—listen with all due respect I come from a cul-de-sac that is like every other two car garage, tinted radio a partial square and the local herd just on the outskirt, and no I never attended the herd, I was either assisting in the house duties or at confession. as far as the local practitioner I told this gentleman of the words of the st. alexandria, I listen in fear of my life how does the unheard send either a saint or martyr of antioch tell me . . . you tell me, who else could I turn to but my local practitioner, the rest of the world perhaps? do you think I am crazy spending my days in prayer instead of my portal information system, your questions seem to have little to do with my purpose here. I am telling you I had a vision that I must tell the one who knows to save us all.

the middle looked like all the others only foozled in time and without a muscle movement

—is it true you left your town at an early age to pray at the shrine of the martyrs, is it true and why would you leave, why?

—it doesn't matter, prayer is prayer, and yes I went to the shrine only to get away from the noise of the town, only there in the still did the voices come.

—and what of these voices, when did you first hear them?

—*I was in my thirteenth year*, it was a *voice to guide me . . . I seldom hear it without light*.

just then or moments on either side a wave of soft still caressed the room as the faces of custodians of nature lost their spongy taboo feel and became almost human in a blessed manner. the touch of the light lay its hand on my bones that relaxed into timeless crescent — over and over it would be the same thing — my voices would tell me trust in the universe and soon I would be at the end of new sovereign and beyond.

the question keeps reproducing questions out of magic hats, rabbits were replaced by other questions with homes of questions where question would drive the new convertible questions around the neighborhood. that came speeding right out of that haze towards me without lights on.

——was it true you broke your contract for marriage?

——were you a member in good standing of the citizens standing committee?

coming at me like unheard orders shipped and sold to the front lines, but I was no longer there, floating above, a light had descended, a light that held me with hands that comforted the hands that held the original spark in a palm of reflection comforting small capillaries from the cold and then without a knock at the door before me was my voice and below I was answering questions that bounded back and forth like artillery vexations. it wasn't me, it was my voice, it was me, it was my voice, it was the voice that was me that had come to me to let me know time was critical as these lovers of rat traps went on with no end to their rummaging rampage as I floated with my head in the warmth of universal backlit recessed fluorescents. days folded into millions of miniscule particles that floated just above a state of perpetual absolution, or it could have been time for lunch when I landed in my body and the head prosecutor looked through me unannounced.

—this is enough for today, please return tomorrow. remember tomorrow is a fasting day do not eat after prime time we must check your soul for purity and determine which sexual position you would take if asked? you have had sex and know your proper positions don't you?

looking at the head common denominator.

—I am sent here to stop the atrocities before it's too late. sex or not has no bearing on the weather. all you need to know is I am more than suitable to show secrets of an ever expansive soul.

—well, my child, since you are too young to know we must be sure before we let you go to the next level of your examination, as you know we are under budget restraints and you must realize you have yet to tell us what this great secret is, what kind of secret could you have to offer. I do not care that your local past prefect sent a letter of authenticity. you must give us something or you're nothing to us but a nuance wanting to be accented. we are here to find true performers of the sacred and secretarial and not have our time wasted on every so called phantom ghost speculators.

to offer a dog a bone is only out of pity and charm to give away a vision can be nothing more than the twicking sound of the medieval raising its voice.

—I have been sent in part to bring zero language, to support the comeoneinall in doing nothing as the creative response that constitutes the universe in doing so the one who knows but fears so can start the motion moving start the clock rolling down the hill and crash into the holly whatnot that sings in the spring time. don't you know this is bigger than the latest fashion for ken and barbie? I can show the one who knows ways to finally free this idol from worship and stop any further law compounding.

flappy forehead and center stage where a failed suit looks at me through steel beams

—enough child, that's enough for the day is early and remember to fast . . . I will take all under advisement, and remember we are not so much against you as it's our duty to make sure visionaries are. . . .

back again to return again with those who came this way one more time to return again to the next day to domrémy and new sovereign and in an instant and in a step and in a pause came a pause that leaves its heart on the table, between the dishes and peach pits, wondering if it was the wrong number to relinquish oneself at night only to move on to the next plastic seat? encounter no this pause comes from a knock at the door, that could be a message from battle weary paratrooper, or simultaneous conjoined twins in their suffering, now separate voices, with merciful insight. one more item that had to be spoken to these char-broiled beef steaks that grunted and huffed in the question dismount, just one more thought to consider. in the descent of the door facing my jury, the voice light ease into me, next to me, on each side of me, I was in the hands of that that has always been.

—with all your doubt you must know, with all your doubt you must pass on to the one who knows but lives in doubt. this place we are in is not anyone's one and only. it is not ruled by all nightly process, or a switch of the indicator, you would like to think it is or was, or has or always will be, and then we can all go home, lock another one up in the tupperware container, burped seal and ready to freeze. you tell this to the one who knows, I know the fear that straddles the shoulders and boundaries of walls, that seeps in of the color of lead bullets, I know and I see it is not in the one and only's lap, but in the hand of the hands that has led to places and names without names, to bricks and diction free range, though it went through different recipes to finally reach the dream state, we must abandon completely once and for all those nasty side road scavengers, hoof and stone promises. you tell the one who knows that was the universe straightening out the sheets, not some probate indication writing up so called historical fictional characterizations. you tell the one who knows that it has nothing to do with hills and travels, it is only found on antigone's way near the shadow theme, where no answer can be found. you tell the one who knows I am here to bring a message and the message is I know how to release all this and there is no need to keep trying the work has been done, it just takes a moment to listen, and tell the one who knows the message I have, I have a message for the one who knows, deliver that message, through the post office over night express, there is no time to waste, days that are wasted are days when one more dies, and bodies pile up.

one more time I must re-return to the world and inform this as before, it may be another day of road shock sitting or side walk instructions, but I must inform those who judge me there is no time, the urgency is a matter of life and death as the wind crumbles the very flesh that they sit on constructed from an abundance of pork and ale, but they only want to enjoy their cushion and not the truth, so I must return to the ones waiting for me in this indirect light with its static charge running through, where the world loses its shadow, where gold is no longer caught behind a robe or in the spotlight of a holding cell, but in the ever glow that lets fairies relax on the side streets and in shopping malls. as I return to the station to re-re-turn again to return again to stand in hot torment of those that will lose their life to protect me and serve, eternally too high of a cost. how can I tell them, we need to stay one more night in an inn with oily straw to sleep on. how can I tell them, those who take the domrémy line with me dayinnout, only to return again to dirt and accommodation, they know as well as I that this is a sequence to the next, but a necessary one to achieve the one after that.

within the distances of sight I am comforted by an image of choisy greeting me. from my first day here this giant glamor queen approached me, or maybe it was the universe that brought us together. there huddled under the entry way to the universe with the smooth glow of dawn, dressed like one who could have been held in high regard in the medical profession but chose professional tennis as an option. you can spot them a year away, the kind that would go as far as morocco, just to find the right parts, and there without notice, coming to wait for the opening of early tellall and getitoutonthefloor, who came to me without prior notice, who came to me with the guidance of my voices.

—I've heard rumors of you and that you're here to remove the veil, I would like to serve with you in the struggle, since I am also from a place of boxes box cutter, which usually fit horribly, and bleed heavily.

—but how do you know who I am?

—are you not the one you are not?

—yes . . . but, how?

—everyone has heard of you being tested, that you wish to speak to the one who knows . . .

—but lives in fear?

—yes, some call me jan jegenson, or rene eon, you can call me choisy.

there was something about this one who would help me through the centuries, both gentle and slender, sweet and graceful.

—what makes you think you can assist me in freeing the world that lands so hard on the corners of poetry makers?

—*some* have *said I* have *two personalities. my mind tend(s)towards tranquility, solitude and study, but my heart loves* the clash of weapons and display of military drills. I *was unable to consult with men or women, so I consulted with god and the devil and so as to not fall into the water I jumped into the fire,* and now I am here as your servant.

at that moment, the light laid a haze at the place where the voices came and even without consulting them I knew this one was ready to do battle, this one had performed the priestess principle of Cybele, and had worked part time as a guard in a Byzantium harem. this one would be with me till the end of the line.

—what of what you wear, red, maybe a little too much for nationalist testers and meeting off-shoot royals?

—I wear not what is expected, I wear for the indication, it's a matter of what suits me any more than that and it's too much sugar in the cake. there is work to be done here, I must convince the one who knows to single the zero process, and then nothing like you have ever seen. at first everyone will cling to lies as indigestible items, but soon we will see places change from things to verbs and it will be miraculous, but I think you already know that and know what we must do.

—no, silly me, maybe I worry too much how I would fit into any given situation or style *at times I wanted to enter a convent of nuns, at other times I wished to hide beneath the banner of the dragoon (where to tell the truth I'd rather have) the dust of military glory*, but I only tell you this as a secret. the confession will open soon. I do hope for a queenkings to practice my entertainment skills as a way to make a living, I am sure if I could get an agent I could make it, but for now no matter, how I dream, my soul is with you.

I knew after that brief moment I was on my way to turning this around, I also knew they would try to find a box for both of us to fill out, but I know if I could connive those inquisitors I could finally throw these boxes out.

the day was dimming and I was exhausted from hours of testing and days of testing before that, all I wanted was sleep and to pray.

—hurry hurry.

what could it be that choisy was yelling and waving at me from nowhere.

—hurry hurry

I have never seen choisy this excited, pointing in the direction of the old stone that flattened without any shadows and standing just this side of the wooden fort is what appeared to be a steel worker, or maybe some sort of paid mercenary. I wanted a close look to question this individual, I knew that who ever went up against the grammar grid lock would never speak again. as I approached I could see that this one could have been a prior, or a pope or a queenking. just as I was about to greet this fine kernel of truth I noticed a trickle on my face and hair, then another . . . and out of nowhere as if ten million snow flakes descended in a gentle waltz I was surrounded by all the life's butterflies past and future. I dare not move due to their tender nature, there were so many I could hardly see the inn and choisy, just wings, colors I had only seen when the voices came to me, iridescent crimsons, incandescent lotus flowers, luminous saffron, transparent azure, a crystallization of lusters, a flicker of gold and the spirit of ivory. for a minute or so, maybe this was from before or later but the world froze, all but the quiet movement of millions upon millions of tiny winged creatures whispering to my soul and before I could take another breath the last one was gone and the world continued, the dust lay on the earth and I just stood there in the air as choisy and this new body ran towards me.

—you truly are blessed.

said the new one, dressed in armor and on one knee before me.

—I am here to serve you, my name is caeneus, I will ride with you into the path of deification and lay bare their lies with one twist of the blade gotten say so say so.

I whispered.

—*it surely is lesser ignorance to write a word with every consonant too few than add too many* as my voices have told me.

the three of use moved through an edge of silence until we entered the inn for bread and some wine. we could hear the heart speak and remind us of the fire within us. it was a rustic place with wall-to-wall indoor-outdoor flooring, recessed lighting, long near plastic walls everyone has been talking about, every three feet or so models of the idols that could have easily turned into some kind of sacred practice, but these were only models that someone had assembled and stretched some kind of skin over. the rest was rather quiet, except for the three of us there, listening to the piano player, playing an off-beat version of "a very recent invention."

looking around I look at both of them sitting there waiting for the next step.

—*what scared* (us) *all into time? into bodies, into shit? I will tell you: the word*, does any one remember, or does it get piled on with a little spittle here and the tomb of the uncommon there?

I knew the conversation of flying words that flew across the table, doing the jig and with little acknowledgment of what keeps going on and on this phoneme connected to this phoneme was slipping in and out of catching historical facts, points of references and interesting sites where tourists go, lie one spot on the railing at niagara falls where when one looks over the edge, where gravity and the velocity of the water reaches up and rushing by and descending at a million gallons an hour or so or more, grabs one by the perceptual mind, beckoning it to plunge deep into that that rushes over the edge of time, only to be splattered and torn to shreds by the rocks below.

the voices keep bantering back and forth, not my voices but choisy and caeneus, my voice keeps telling me that the paideuma was ready on the oar or not there for turmoil to come forth on the afternoon plane with its intersecting curves with those slight slicker forms and anamght, oh yes I knew this was the ascended to those that had so long laid their burns bared like scarred-over brands, whether on a shingle or a single sneeze, why not just excommunicate those from the salon, or gathers of dreamers, especially the crucial one I would say. it is my lot to take the band wagons to the wall fires and free this as that and as though the night glows fluorescent waves of liquid light circling in for a landing as the voices of choisy and caeneus guide me in with plans and shuffle board scores . . . ah the petty bursts of competition that can turn into reinventions of the ruff righter myths.

—as I was saying I know most of the panelists and am willing to go before them as your witness and protector.

this voice was calling me out along the light beam along with the other?

—are you listening? are you with us? do you have contact or are you with them?

I can never tell from this world and that or when I am here or that it usually takes someone calling my name or an arrow in the foot, but if gay paree needs light and the resistance is failing what can I say?

—yes, yes, yes, I am here, what is it? *let none tomorrow dare to leave the town and go out to fight, unless* (they have*) first go to confession.*

the heat of the hearth caresses my cheek, it is the light of the voices that whisper across my temples.

—yes, yes I am here, what was it you are saying?

caeneus is friends with all the brisk examiners, those duck-n-cover lookers.

— yes, yes and I would like to go with you to the parade to offer what I can offer.

—wonderful idea choisy, yes first thing before we take the domrémy line and beyond we must get to confession.

I knew it was time the voices had come.

—we must hurry before the light changes.

behind me both were trying to stay close.

—hurry we must confess, the light is right.

—the clothes, remember, not the red coat, it must be armor against the world, steel armor, against the iron tip, the gold armor to protect one from sin.

choisy was yelling at me from a distance, even though I knew even before the words were uttered.

the sky was a flat hue with flat detail.

—yes, yes, but we must get to the shrine and give our confession and you two must come along.

—the armor, what about the armor?

one of them spoke or both in a chorus of concern.

—hurry, now, there's no time to spare.

—I . . .

choisy started to cry out something but I already knew.

—yes, yes the armor, you have a suite of armor for me from when you were younger.

—yes, how did you know?

—hurry now, we must get to confession.

at the stone chapel that opened to the universe, I fell to my knee, surrounded by the old stone wall of the round table and the great pyramid bathed in a rich emerald moss, the glow of dusk, the moon, the stars. I could feel the earth soak though my flesh. I could hear choisy and caeneus breathing heavy behind me.

—on your knees and open yourself to the dust of the universe, the dust of life, let it settle on your eye lids, let in stories of creation.

just then the north star seemed to increase in volume, I could hear the light whisper to me, the light that had traveled too many years just to speak a few words, words that cradled my soul.

—but goddess, shouldn't we prepare?

stopping my meditation I turned to choisy who was on one knee.

—get down on both knees and never use word in vain, this is a holy universe, pride and ego only set up piles that stick together, confess, confess and pray after me.

> on the field of grass of grain of pleasure, on the field of yesteryear tomorrow and the next one to come, on the field bloodied with too many nouns, on the field and on the cracked sidewalk up to the donotcross, to the grassy knoll bunker hill, to the plain old gray lost between black and white's fleshy

decisions running down the workers back on the tip of a salamander. on the field, on the plains that were oceans, that settled on the leaf leftovers to dry from the steel blade — *think feeling, they feel tempting, they tempt daring, they dare waiting, they wait taking, they take thanking*, past the yellow flashing to the field uncut or spread eagle soaring like winches case coming not to roust this cast lost, and on a first drop that was never more from the bone and clatter to the endless and eternal winds. allten allten and allten.

after the night had settled and gone away. after the morning light had ben readjusted. after dressing in armor that caeneus offered, shining and ready to do battle with proverbs and pronouns, armor so close to my body to feel sexual, a form fitting metal chest plate, after the bullet proof vest, after the chain mail, after the knee cap spikes, after being covered with glistening alloys of composite features, with a sort of ornamental post mortem mannerist display of everything inlaid in gold along the broader area.

I felt like a mythical figure born in the castration of the sea. I was ready, we were ready, ready to take the domrémy line to new sovereign and beyond to begin again.

I walked in the silence of afterthoughts, in vision I approach the light as does everyone. in this vision I always rest, it's not so much light as the comfort of a flicker from the fluorescent on the local. bathed in a sermon without words. after taking our red plastic seats and jerked into forward motion leaving some forever behind. we sit in silence as we did this morning, as we did while we dressed and applied our steel plating, as we did when we went through the turn style, as we did when we sat in what we know that wasn't spoken, as we sat the night before in the future and in the end that would never end.

in the still, I imagined a piece of metal or more than one piece enter my flesh, I imagined the armor I am not wearing that is a decent suit for mass transportation, or long trips on tall black either or both in silence, metal entering my body, I will mark the day, mark the spot where the metal came in and exited on the way to hell, I will mark the entry wound on this imagined armor, on these red plastic seats of the domrémy to new sovereign and beyond.

the question and answer were taking place in an atmosphere of doused light, the grand inquisitor was playing a game show host, because I was flanked by a warrior queenking and a devoted swash-buckling killer, but devotion for one hundred seemed to be a formality.

—what mythical object was used with thirteen knots from patirt's passion to artaud . . .

—a . . . (could hear the music build), a . . . cane?

—you are right for one hundred points. our next category for three hundred points . . .

enough, I have to stop this infection that is spreading on the surface like radioactive pond scum.

—I must speak to the one who knows, but lives in fear, I know there will be second sight and the walls, rooms, prerogatives of life can be assaulted and we can start anew. it is not me you understand, but the voices that come through me from the beginning of time or the grain of sand all the drops of water that ever fell, none can be spoken from and none defined. I am only the vehicle for the energy to pass through me. you must let me pass and continue to this path of freedom.

there was hand waving, lights flashing, the image of a concierge draped in velveteen waded through to center stage and before this hogwild titfortat hostess with the mostess would gurgle I responded.

—we have no time to waste, one hour, one more day stationed in one more year that sets up this assembly line of carnage, one more second is the second a causality is created, one more second that we waste here not bringing the voices of the universe to the one who knows but lives in fear, one more second before the trains arrive at the domrémy to new sovereign and beyond to take us further than there.

2.

    I woke to see early morning window shadows create a stronger purpose,
    marked by perfectly snapped objects.
    along to new sovereign and beyond to the earth dome done and done.

    past command past flesh tattoos
    past chattel on work release emancipation

    past the watchers who watch the instituted distinguish one from the other

    past a long ocean that lays in route neglect
    past nine digit numbers that hush the fringe
    past camps on pages and off
    past I know them not how they breathe or plead, but by index   trigger

past shadow hole huddles where proper names light is a short
fuse

it hadn't been a long trip, but for some their first time traveling hundreds of hours or miles, and others the first site of a castle that was the castle for a day until another came along preferably with updated versions of wooden bridges and the like. it was a sight to hold on to as long as one could, warriors, workers all there to maintain what my voices told me was a lie and what I knew the one who knows knows to be a lie.

proceeding towards the entry we are met by guards, secret service agents that are not there, host to the royal hoster of royal events, who informed me that the others must wait and only I would be allowed to enter.

I could tell by the looks and murmurs I was anticipated with mixed reviews. this pair of military was undisciplined and maybe not too bright since they all must have thought I was deaf. I could hear their glossarial ooze from loosened lips.

—here to save the day, ay? that would be us, more to the point.

—just a peasant trying to get a leg up on the competition, I'd say.

my voices must have been watching over me as these midnight cowhoots wanted to play trip the one who doesn't play by their rules. I was able to glide over their intended obstacle course with ease. I felt a certain sadness leaving this lot of check mate warriors, for I knew they would be under my command, their blood would seep into the dirt and rivers of my life. it seemed better to let them have one more bohemian on Broadway with the camaraderie huddle around the fake fire, drinking ale, chewing fibrous protein just to warm themselves before long cold assaults still their blood. it may be their last hour staring into each other's eyes with that passionless look one gets when one is asking for casual sex.

I continued to follow my twinkle with the mostess to the great hall where I was surrounded by eight carnivorous guards. I felt like a rock star, a martyr, or someone on their way to death row.

proceeding along a corridor we were joined by black suited, sunglassed individuals whose armor clinked as we marched along, and there before me seeping out of the entry was the oily lights of a spectacle about to be turned on with sun rise blindness. the sound was a roar seeping from behind thick stone walls, with the after vibrations dancing through the mortar and rock like the afterglow of fire works. the room was lubricated with the buzz of inebriation.

my own anticipation grew as a generator gaining momentum to electrify an entire city. the guards, walking shoulder-to-shoulder. with each step the lights became sprinklers of electrical glee, the room was filled with slingshot echoes conversations seeping in and out of a primal ooze of chit chat. I knew that it was no longer just me and the voices of the universe, it was no longer me conversing with those that could never be that exist in every speck of dust and in every corner and crevasse of the thoughts of that dust. I belonged to the vastness of space and I was only a conduit for possibilities, a super conductor, a parenthesis. I was the lens on the hubble telescope. the hulls of rice, the breath of a whisper. I was no longer here being corralled by a security force, my atoms dispersed. I was approaching my egypt, my new sovereign and beyond. I was entering the vaginal cavity of my birth, moist and salty, oozing in the original spark, one great process to the cataclysm, calcium deposit dripping in a careless rhythm over and over clocked in at the forty billionth drop on a ten mile high phosphorescent stalagmite.

   the cavity approaches, I approach the cavity. I make out faces conversing with other faces lit in brilliant hope. the hollow opens to a large atrium whose parts are dismissed by distance times space to the power of infinity. the atmosphere an air apparent encased in a background seeped gluey lute melodies snaking through silk furrieries, lingering on the outer miasmic edge of perfumes and aromatic food in caravel abundance. this was the elite not out of disposition to their status, but loose enough to animate bodies lived in fear. here is a moment of gravity, a moment when one could pass on the latest gossip and be it at the same time, as a warm summer breeze radios through tender leaves and the dead live on in generational memento mori.

   as my ever encasing entourage enters this buoyant atmosphere there is at first a breath's pause away from normal, a gasp, a hesitation spark that spreads over the convergence as one slowly applies the pressure to a window pane, at first you hear the tiny particle letting go of their conviction then out of weakness a crack appears and spreads shock wave fractures from ground zero, a pebble loosens in the wind and creates a landslide leading to a chain reaction of heads turning towards me in a distilled silent shill, frozen in the tick of a second, millennia to millennia to the next click, lead then marble, ancient roman concrete, rigid as death and twice as quiet. the parade continues though paused only momentarily by the present pause, by the immeasurable stillness that creases the air into pleated scenarios. then the red sea becomes a repeat performance, this intercourse that had been put on stasis with fixated eyes slowly parts, not in neat symmetrical order, but as if by magnetic pull, all the particles are drawn to the opposite side as a passage way of human beings parts to create an envelope that I am dropped dead center towards someone in a darkened all-purpose posed chair, a figure not there.

—I have come with a message from the universe to raise a siege against lists and proper behavior.

in the shadow a figure leaned out enough to pass judgments and waved me forth.

as I proceeded towards this shadow camera flashes jumped at me from the darkness, at the same time I could see others holding small crutches around their necks, holy water, or sacred toil, I perquire. then as the voices had stopped they started again in lullaby electronics, inconsequential at first, a drop of water on a tin roof, a slow tap dance after the harangue is gone home and it's just you and the dancer with a body of the never best. then as castor oil was seemingly rubbed into tactless minds, the random switch was turned on, pennies from heaven, grains of sand, bees gathering for the union meeting, all turning into a sound mass for hushed voices, a collaboration between john cage and the sidekick cabaret voltaire arkestra. in hushed jabberwocky heads were turning just enough to acknowledge the ones they were talking to, but never quite enough to take their eyes completely off me. a continuous melody of head movements and subtle finger pointers filtered through rustling interjections created by a human corridor that widens and leads to the one who knows but lives in fear.

to this first step I take that has been promised since so many before me have taken that same step with: "m" names, "g" names, "l" names, "j" names and "x" names and so on, uttered that often repeated idiom: "let my be godspeak" where what got into in the choice of until we get to the here and relays the depth that this reshuffled cannibal talk has to be dismantled, the claustrophobic haze wiped away to resemble simple primal guttural sound and sexual innuendoes placed on the skin instead of being perverted with long-winded hey babe wanta come over and see my ethics, my new large being, my here to eternity list of turds that conquered the world.

and so I continued down this fleshy container surrounded by guard arms and courtly hush tones complete with click track and a slight echo. within the time it takes for me to look forward and blink and be further forward I was aware of the lavish outfit ahead of me, and then I stop say again,

—in the name of everything . . . I have come to give a sign to the one who knows, I have come to help raise a siege against those forces that grasp labels with bloodied stumps just to receive their months' disablement checks, I am here to tell the one who knows I have a sign for now and for that one only, I am here to tell you why I am here sent to you on this day, but you give me a fake device, a dupe, an actor-governor . . . I am here with the path we must take and you play joke-arama with your destiny . . . do you hear me I am here to show us set us there and there but I can't do it on my own.

the room was put into a jar, the room solid with the immobile, just then a butterfly happened to be in the upper reaches of the early morning rays, making its way through the dust particles towards me and just as it got eye level, there before me.

—you are the one I am sent by the universe and stars . . . *I offer good health to you.*

with a glance away as if I was talking to the person in either the left or other left side or maybe three rows behind.

—it is not I, oh me you must have the wrong one, I am just an attachment to the place over there on the other side, you must mean someone else, the one you want waits for you up there.

—this is the utmost concern and yet you volley with me, I know you are the one, but I also know you are fearful of being the one.

with a look betraying discovery, I knew and I fell to my knees.

—I am here to offer myself to you as I offer my soul to the universe.

—I have heard of your way that . . . all this way with guard arms from inquisition center

. . . yes I hear you are here to right the amazon and save the earth, is that it and do you take what you truly have?

—I am only the one who brings the message of voices in concrete from the other reaches of time itself.

—and these voices, what do they say . . . we all want to hear . . . any good jokes from the fringes, from the blue shift moments? please what do these voices say . . . we all want to hear.

communal clicking spread through those gathered as voices went from single click here and there, the popping of release values held tight in fear, to a paranoid chatter, as a reflected outside of the inside or maybe paranormal communiqués from within looking for a place to stay, to say, to find a ground in the other, other than clicking performance response designed for the one charged with a measure that everything is measured against in kindly supportive — we are all here to serve and make you happy. I am sure if it was something other than crack filler, there would not be so much click and clatter but more . . . .

—oh please tell us, you say you are here to save us, certainly you want to save us all, not just you and me . . . how would that look, you and me on a deserted island or a desert, how would that look after the big pomp and circumstances comes along and it's you and me on some atoll in the south sea or some oasis mirage because we knew and we were saved because we knew. not very cordial of you to keep a secret like that. oh please tell us what pill we need to take or what mantra to proclaim, don't hold back . . . we are all waiting, please hurry, please we can't wait.

    the crowd turned into a serendipitous carnival, sending generous gaffes on a silver platter to the one who knows with an increasing surrender, modulated by two factors. one, whether they were laughing with the one who knows or two, at me. still, this sanguine crowd covered in plastic jewels seems to glance my way with their side eyes as a smirk and chuckle was imitated from their pursed lips.

notes

2   *I saw the fire lighted . . .*
    These are Joan's words from her trial on Wednesday, May 23, 1431: "If I were at the place of execution, and I saw the fire lighted, and the faggots catching and the executioner ready to build up the tire, and if I were in the tire, even so I would say nothing else, and I would maintain what I have said at this trial until death. I have nothing more to say" (William Trask, *Joan of Arc in Her Own Words*. [New York: Turtle Point, 1996], 132).

2   *the day the earth stood still*
    Later in the manuscript, edwards quotes from the movie *The Day the Earth Stood Still*.

4   *and there . . . from within . . .*
    These are Joan's words from her trial on May 2, 1431: "You will not do what you say against me without suffering for it both in body and soul" (Trask 131).

4   *on the blood red trickling . . .*
This text is a quote from Julian of Norwich, another female mystic. This was her last vision before her death:
> Suddenly I saw the red blood trickling from under the crown, all hot, flowing freely and copiously, a living stream, just as it seemed to me that it was at the time when the crown of thrones was thrust down upon his blessed head. Just so did he, both God and man, suffer for me. I perceived, truly and powerfully, that it was himself who showed this to me, without any intermediary.

(Julian of Norwich, *Showings*, trans. Edmund Colledge OSA and James Walsh SJ [New York: Paulist, 1978], 126.)

4   *long tumultuous shouting sounds . . .*
From Edgar Allan Poe, *The Fall of the House of Usher* [Heraklion, 2014].

5   *I would rather die . . .*
Joan was wounded during the siege of Orléans. When some offered to charm her wound, she said those words to them. (Trask 37)

5   *I could sufer more . . .*
I have not been able to locate the source of these lines.

6   *If I should say the heavens . . .*
After Joan revokes her abjuration, she says: "If I should say that God had no sent me, I should damn myself. It is true that God has sent me" (Trask 138).

6   *the furrows which have made a bed . . .*
"See the furrows, which have traced a bed for themselves on my colourless cheeks; they are the drop of blood and the drop of

sperm which flow along my dry wrinkles." (Isadore Ducasse, Comte de Lautréamont, *Les Chants de Maldoror*, trans. Joyce Ridley and Francis Scarfe, in *Contemporary Poetry and Prose*, ed. Roger Roughton [London: Frank Cass and Company Limited, 1968], 110.)

6   *I protest against being kept . . .*
Testimony from Joan's trial. God was changed to the heavens by edwards. "I come, sent by God," is the original quote. (Trask 93, 95)

7   *the enola gay*
Enola Gay was a B-29 that "dropped an atomic bomb on the military port of Hiroshima on August 6, 1945. The heat and blast effaced everything in the vicinity, burned 4.4 square miles, and killed some 70,000 people (lingering injuries and radiation sickness brought the death toll past 100,000 by the end of the year)." ("Enola Gay." *Encyclopædia Britannica*. Web. 8 Mar 2016.)

7   *if you were to have me torn limb from limb . . .*
When Joan is threatened by torture, she says: "Truly, if you were to have me torn limb from limb and send my soul out of my body, I would say nothing else. And if I did say anything, afterwards I should always say that you had made me say it by force" (Trask 132).

7   *as for signs . . .*
"As for signs, if those who ask for one are not worthy of it, I am not accountable for that" (Trask 125–26).

7   *klaatu barata nikto*
A famous phrase from the 1951 sci-fi movie *The Day the Earth Stood Still*.

8   *I do my best to serve . . . I was sent by the heavens.*
      All of the italics text in this section comes from the various parts of Joan's testimony.

12   *listening to the flicker . . .*
      I was not able to locate the source of this quotation. As I wrote in the previous chapter, edwards usually indicates that the text is a quotation from somewhere else by putting it in italics. The use of quotation marks here and in a couple of other places in the manuscript is thus unusual.

16   *I do not know a from b*
      Joan to her examiners, as she was trying to get an audience with the Dauphin: "I do not know A from B. I am come from the King of Heaven to raise the siege of Orléans and to lead the Dauphin to Reims to be crowned and anointed" (Trask 25).

16   *rather . . . sit and sew . . .*
      February, 1429. Joan's words at her lodging to Jean de Metz: "Far rather would I sit and sew beside my poor mother, for this thing is not my condition. But I must go, and I must do this thing, because my Lord will have it so" (Trask 15–16).

16   *rather now than tomorrow . . .*
      Again, Joan's words to Jean de Metz: "Rather now than tomorrow, and tomorrow than the day after!" (Trask 16)

16   *twice and thrice a week . . .*
      Joan, talking about her childhood and how she was first visited by "a voice from God" (Trask 5): "Twice and thrice a week the voice told me that I must depart and go into France" (Trask 8).

20 *I was in my thirteenth year . . .*
"When I was thirteen, I had a voice from God to help me to govern myself. The first time, I was terrified. The voice came to me about noon. It was summer, and I was in my father's garden. I had not fasted the day before. I heard the voice on my right hand, towards the church. There was a great light all about" (Trask 5).

26 *an image of choisy*
choisy indicates François-Timoléon de Choisy (1644–1724), a writer whose father had a connection to the household of the Duke of Orléans and whose mother was an intimate friend of Anne of Austria. According to Choisy's memoir, his mother dressed him as a girl until he was eighteen, and after a brief pause, he later resumed dressing as a woman himself. I write more on choisy in the introduction.

27 *jan jegenson*
Most likely an allusion to Christine Jorgensen, the first American trans person who came out publicly as transgender and whose transition was highly publicized.

27 *rene eon*
choisy uses words from "Charles, chevalier d'Éon de Beaumont, (born Oct. 5, 1728, Tonnerre, Fr. — died May 21, 1810, London), French secret agent from whose name the term 'eonism,' denoting the tendency to adopt the costume and manners of the opposite sex, is derived." ("Charles, chevalier d'Éon de Beaumont." *Encyclopædia Britannica*. Web. 8 Mar 2016.) I write more about d'Eon in the introduction.

28 *some have said I have two personalities . . .*
"I had two personalities. My mind tended toward tranquility, solitude, and study. Prudence told me that this was the wisest and

~59~

simplest way to shield myself, but my heart loved the clash of weapons and the display of all the military drills. Unable to consult either man or woman, I consulted God and the Devil, and, so as not to fall into the water, I jumped into the fire." (Charles d'Eon de Beaumont, *The Maiden of Tonnerre: The Vicissitudes of the Chevalier and the Chevalière d'Eon*, trans. Roland A. Champagne, Nina Claire Ekstein, and Gary Kates [Baltimore: The Johns Hopkins University Press, 2004], 7.)

28 *Cybele*
Anatolian earth goddess; ancient goddess of fertility; in Rome, she was known as Magna Mater (Great Mother).

29 *at times I wanted to enter a convent of nuns . . .*
From d'Eon de Beaumont:
> Contradictory resolutions troubled me day and night. At times I wanted to enter the convent of nuns, at other time I wished to hide beneath the banner of the dragoons, for which I had great propensity ever since my youth, when I had been excited by the uniform, the horses, and the military drills of La Rochefoucault's dragoon regiment, which had its winter quarters in my native Tonnerre. (7)

31 *caeneus*
Caenis is a female character in Ovid's Metamorphoses, who, according to her wish, is transformed by Neptune from female to male (Caeneus) after being raped by him. As a male, Caeneus is also invulnerable to weaponry. See more on Caeneus in the introduction.

31 *it is surely lesser ignorance . . .*
"And it is surely a lesser ignorance to write a word with every consonant too few than to add all too many." (James Joyce,

Finnegans Wake, ed. Robert-Jan Henkes, Erik Bindervoet, and Finn Fordham [Oxford: Oxford University Press, 2012], 115.)

32   *what scared (us) all into time? . . .*
"What scared you all into time? Into body? Into shit? I will tell you: '*the word*.'" (William Burroughs, *Nova Express* [New York: Grove, 2011], 4.)

33   *paideuma*
Term that German ethnologist and archeologist Leo Frobenius used to describe the way in which culture imprints itself on humans. Ezra Pound used the word similarly, but for him it meant a cultural template (including biases, habits of thinking, etc.) that people carry inside them. It is basically something that cannot be learned but is inherent through cultural norms.

33   *anamght*
Word indecipherable.

34   *let none tomorrow dare to leave . . .*
Joan to her chaplain on Ascension Eve, May 4, 1429: "Let none tomorrow dare to leave the town and go out to fight, unless he has first gone to confession. And let them beware lest women of evil fame follow them: because, for sin, God will permit the loss of this war" (Trask 35).

37   *think feeling, they feel tempting . . .*
Joyce 142.

39   *thirteen knots*
It is believed that a hangman's knot should have thirteen coils; since thirteen is an unlucky number, this symbolizes the destiny of those about to be hanged.

39   *patirt's passion*
     In edwards' manuscript "patirts passion," but I was not able to locate the reference.

39   *artaud*
     Antonin Artaud was a French dramatist, developer of the "theater of cruelty." He was also an actor and played Jean Massieu, a court bailiff at Joan's trial, in Carl Theodor Dreyer's 1928 silent film *The Passion of Joan of Arc*.

43   *2.*
     In edwards' document, this section follows the previous one, also marked as "2." Either this section is from a different part of the manuscript, or edwards made a mistake in numbering the sections.

49   *a collaboration between . . .*
     edwards makes several allusions here — to John Cage, Cabaret Voltaire, The Sun Ra Arkestra, and Lewis Caroll's poem "Jabberwocky."

kari edwards (1954–2006) was a poet, artist, and gender activist born 523 years after Joan of Arc was burned at the stake. edwards' book *succubus in my pocket* (EOAGH Books, 2015) was the winner of the 2015 Lambda Literary Award for Transgender Poetry. edwards was a Small Press Traffic book of the year award winner (2004) and a recipient of New Langston Arts Bay Area Award in literature (2002). edwards is the author of *bharat jiva* (Litmus Press, 2009); *having been blue for charity* (Blazevox, 2007); *obedience* (Factory School, 2005); *iduna* (O Books, 2003); *a day in the life of p.* (subpress collective, 2002); *a diary of lies* (Belladonna Chapbooks #27, Belladonna, 2002); and *POST/(PINK)* (Scarlet Press, 2000).

Tina Žigon is an Assistant Professor of English at American University of Kuwait. Originally from Maribor, Slovenia, she moved to Kuwait via San Marcos, Texas, where she earned her MA in Literature at Texas State University, and Buffalo, New York, where she earned her PhD in Literature at the University at Buffalo–SUNY. Her dissertation is titled "'Language Out of Bounds': Gender, Language, and Violence in kari edwards' *a day in the life of p.* and the Joan of Arc Project."

www.ingramcontent.com/pod-product-compliance
Lightning Source LLC
Chambersburg PA
CBHW070849160426
43192CB00012B/2363